What Our Readers Have Said...

"Although I consider myself a seasoned sales professional, it is helpful to have past learning's refreshed. The books were also beneficial because of the information concerning 'trends' in the sales relationship. The sales process should be viewed as dynamic since business relationships change regularly."

•

"For the particular business I am in and the type of sales calls I have, I find that the books in the Pinpoint Sales Training Series are very often applicable to how I conduct business. I would recommend them to other sales people, just not ones that are in my industry."

•

"These books provide very good concepts. It fits in well with the Bell Leadership training program that I attended in November."

•

"I use this material in these books and apply it to my customers and other employees I work with."

•

"I would like to know other topics. Is there anything on Production Management or Consultative Selling or Time Management?"

•

"These books are great tools that should be used as guidelines for our everyday

supervisory practices. You need to take the time to do a short self-evaluation when reading them."

•

"The Pinpoint Training Series delivers information that could be used in a lot different areas."

•

"I like this because I can take them with me to read at a convenient time. I feel the little time I have to spend in the office is best use on activities that directly relate to revenue opportunities. I like the short amount of time it takes to keep up with these."

•

"I prefer the self-study approach; it fits in with my schedule."

•

"My thought is that the real value of these books comes into effect when doing the action plans."

•

"Short and sweet. These books are easy to comprehend."

•

"I have enjoyed reading these books. They are relevant to today's work environment and the ongoing change in the way we manage our workforce."

•

"I do feel that these books have been very helpful to me at my job."

•

"I think a lot of the recommendations in these books are very useful, and can be applicable to everyday situations. If nothing else, it's a good reference guide to fall back upon if a situation arises in the future."

•

"These books are relevant to today's work environment and the ongoing change in the way we manage our workforce."

•

Recovering Lost Business

Pinpoint Sales Skill Development Training Series

TIMOTHY F. BEDNARZ

MAJORIUM
BUSINESS PRESS

Pinpoint Sales Skill Development Training Series
"Recovering Lost Business"
Timothy F. Bednarz

Graphic design: Monika Pawlak

Majorium Business Press
2025 Main Street
Stevens Point, WI 54481
715.342.1018 • 800.654.4935

ISBN 978-1-882181-73-5

Printed in the United States of America

Introduction

The Pinpoint Sales Skill Development Training Series is designed for targeted training and education regarding increased improvement in a specific skill or competency.

Each book within this series is designed to be easy to use, understand and apply to your job. It can be used as a basis for training individuals, as a discussion guide or as a personal training tool.

Each chapter within this book discusses a specific concept. When you have completed all eight chapters you should have a 360° perspective of the topic.

Additionally, each chapter is divided into specific sections:

- The first section provides you with an overview of the topic
- The Implications section discusses why the concept is important, and why it is important to learn and apply.
- The Strategies, Tips & Techniques to Apply section teaches how to use and apply the particular concept to your work.
- The Points to Ponder section gives you something to think about or to be discussed with a group setting. These are questions not meant to be immediately answered, but to be pondered over time.
- The Training Activity section provides you with the tools to transfer what you have learned to your job. It is designed to help create an action plan to effectively apply the concept.

Each of the topics in this series is time-tested and proven in the marketplace. They have been used by thousands of employees as training tools. Many of the users have commented that what made these books valuable, was the ability to refer to them when a problem surfaced. They indicated that they remembered reading about the exact problem. They referred back to these books and found an appropriate solution.

You will find them equally valuable as a resource in your professional development library.

Table of Contents

LEARNING OBJECTIVES:

- To understand the reasons and causes of lost business.
- To identify high risk prospects and customers.
- To determine proper responses to losing an account.
- To identify reasons for the loss of business.
- To apply techniques to recover lost business.
- To develop long term strategies to redevelop a lost account.

1

There Are Many Ways to Lose Business

When salespeople think of losing business, they might initially think of a major account or bid being lost to a competitor. However, there are many other ways their customer base can be at risk, especially when the economy slows down and sales soften.

IMPLICATIONS — WHAT THIS MEANS TO YOU

During tenuous times, the salesperson's book of customers is at a higher risk than ever before. If they fail to take the time to protect their business, a minor mistake can be costly, not only in terms of lost commissions, but also in lost profits and increased costs to their company.

As it costs approximately five times more to get new business than it does to keep existing accounts, it makes more sense for salespeople to take the time and effort to hold on to what they already have than to risk going out into an increasingly barren economic landscape to search for new business.

STRATEGIES, TIPS & TECHNIQUES TO APPLY

Salespeople need to recognize that all of their business can be at risk in an unstable economy. There are a number of factors that can affect one's book of business during the year. These include:

Uncontrolled Events

Certain events over which salespeople have no control—bankruptcies, plant closings, relocation and lay offs—can affect their existing business. If a major account closes or goes bankrupt, or if it lays off employees and reduces capacity, the volume of business a salesperson can do with them can be greatly reduced.

While the events shaping future relationships with customers cannot be controlled, salespeople can identify the accounts that are at risk. If they stay on top of industry news, changes and trends that can impact their customers, most uncontrollable events can be anticipated and identified.

Increased Competition

During slow economic periods, competition will greatly intensify. The available pool of current and potential customers will shrink as everyone is out in the market looking to replace lost business. This can also mean the competition becomes increasingly erratic and irrational: some may greatly reduce their prices to buy market share, gladly trading dollars for profits just to keep their doors open.

Increased competition can put more proposals at risk. Competitors may add considerable incentives or start price wars to get new business. As such, salespeople should make it their business to develop as much current competitive information as they can in order to successfully position themselves and their offerings. They should also look for new competitors who might be expanding into their market, as many large competitors who might not have affected them in the past can be reaching for more of the smaller customer base to make up for their losses.

Reduced Quality and Service

To reduce expenses, a salesperson's own company might make strategic moves that affect both the quality of the product and service. Customers may become increasingly dissatisfied with the quality they are receiving, especially when they may be paying more for less.

The potential impact of changes in the salesperson's own company on their customers means that now is the time to fight for their business by staying proactive and in touch to ensure they remain satisfied. Immediate action should be taken to rectify problems the moment they first appear, and customers educated about alternatives to the products they are currently buying. Quality and consistency should be maintained at all costs.

POINTS TO PONDER — SOMETHING TO THINK ABOUT

1. How much of your existing sales base is experiencing problems due to current economic conditions?
2. Have you been able to identify potential opportunities that have presented themselves because of the existing economic conditions? Explain.

TRAINING ACTIVITY — APPLICATION & ACTION PLAN

Review your existing list of customers.

1. Identify the customers that are at risk due to uncontrollable events, increased competition and reduced quality.
2. For every customer that you have identified to be at risk, develop a sales strategy to stabilize the account where possible.
3. For the customers determined to be at risk due to uncontrollable events, identify other sources of potential business to replace these losses.

2

Why Do We Lose Business?

Research demonstrates that most businesses naturally lose 25% of their customer base. Other more recent studies have increased that number to as high as 50%.

Every company experiences a turnover in business for a variety of reasons. However, as companies examine the impact of lost accounts, it has become obvious that it is a good practice to fight to retain current business.

IMPLICATIONS — WHAT THIS MEANS TO YOU

The loss of any business can seriously impact a salesperson. Not only is there the obvious loss of income and commissions, but residual emotional and psychological effects can also impact their overall performance. There is nothing more disheartening than for an individual to work hard to get a new account or maintain a major piece of business only to lose it. Even though the customer's decision is normally a business decision based on simple economics, the salesperson cannot help but take it personally. A natural slump occurs in their sales performance until they are able to overcome the personal defeat.

STRATEGIES, TIPS & TECHNIQUES TO APPLY

As was previously stated, the loss of business is normally a decision based upon the economics facing the customer. Some of the facts involved in the decision are controllable; some are completely out of the salesperson's control. Below is an examination of the most common causes and what the salesperson can do to counter them:

Economic Conditions

Currently, the biggest single business concern is the economy. After almost two decades of sustained economic growth in the 80s and 90s, the business cycle has turned downward. Most current salespeople and managers have never experienced this before and many don't know how to handle it.

There are many things salespeople can control; the economy is not one of them. If customers are reluctant to make major purchases during an economic slowdown, there is little one can do. However, there are some alternatives that might alleviate some of the pain. Salespeople can look for opportunities to expand their business with a major customer with additional products and value-added services. Also, this is an excellent time to look for ways to shift customers to more profitable products. While salespeople may not be able to get any new business, they can certainly increase their overall profit margin. Finally, there will be opportunities for companies to sell their products and services as alternatives to higher-priced products a customer is buying from a competitor.

Pricing

Whether with a new customer or an existing account, pricing can become more of an issue. While a real problem to many companies, pricing is an issue that is within the control of the salesperson.

When a customer perceives all products to be the same, they automatically view them as commodity items and begin to shop for the lowest price. Certain customers will always shop for the lowest price despite valid reasons to do otherwise. However, most customers are more interested in the value received than the price. It is the salesperson's responsibility to educate the customer about the features of their products and services and to demonstrate the value that these represent in both tangible and intangible benefits. A salesperson can use value analysis to demonstrate the per-unit cost to use their product and the savings a customer will realize in productivity, efficiency and profitability.

Quality

A customer might change vendors or choose a competitor's offer on the basis of quality. If a company is experiencing quality problems with their products, this is an event out of the salesperson's control. However, with the rapid changes fueled by technology, the life cycles of many products have been greatly diminished. New products and services are constantly being introduced, and it's up to the salesperson to be aware of both what his or her company is offering and what is being introduced into the market. If they are not prepared to provide the customer with the best available option, they risk losing them to a competitive product.

A pitfall many salespeople encounter is to review what a customer is already buying from a competitor and counter with a similar product, rather than offering a superior product with clearly demonstrable value. The salesperson who is able to evaluate a customer and provide solutions that make operations more efficient, reduce operating costs, and increase performance will be difficult to defeat.

If salespeople experience problems with their own products or services, they must take action to immediately rectify the problem or be able to quickly shift the customer to a better-performing product.

POINTS TO PONDER — SOMETHING TO THINK ABOUT

1. What has been your reaction to lost business? How does it impact your personal sales performance? Explain.
2. In your personal opinion, what is the primary reason you have lost major accounts?

TRAINING ACTIVITY – APPLICATION & ACTION PLAN

Review your A, B and C accounts for the past year, but especially for the last six months.

1. Identify the accounts that you have lost and detail the primary causes of lost business, such as economic conditions, pricing, quality or other factors.
2. Based upon your assessment, determine if the lost business was within your control.
3. If it was, determine a strategy to regain the lost business.

3

Are Your Customers at Risk?

As of the early 2000s, customers are at higher risk than ever before. In previous years when the economy was robust, the biggest risk was posed by the competition. With the slowdown in the economy, new risk factors have been added to the equation. Even when on the surface a customer appears to be healthy, they can be impacted by decisions from corporate headquarters. These decisions can trigger layoffs, slowdowns and plant closings.

Additionally, competition is even more ruthless than before as they attempt to regain lost business and market share.

IMPLICATIONS — WHAT THIS MEANS TO YOU

Salespeople must not be caught unawares by increased economic and competitive risk. They must be attuned to the subtle and not so subtle changes in their industries, territories, markets, and customers. These changes point directly to the customers who are at risk.

Salespeople are always on the hunt for new business. In these economic times, not only do they have to become more aggressive to make up for the losses they are experiencing, but they must also be on the defensive to protect and maintain their own customer base. A sudden downturn in the economy quickly changes the rules, and the faster a salesperson recognizes this and reacts, the better able they will be to weather economic storms.

STRATEGIES, TIPS & TECHNIQUES TO APPLY

There are two main types of risks that a salesperson must recognize. As stated, during a regular business cycle, the most prominent risk is from the competition. This is where the normal sales game is played with product differentiation, features, benefits and pricing. In the current business cycle, the economic risks have increased considerably as well.

Economic Risks

Economic risks can be more treacherous and difficult to identify. A single company locale can be doing well only to be impacted by corporate decisions to consolidate or economize, which then blindsides the salesperson. There are several actions that salespeople can take to stay on top of these threats:

- Changes in ordering patterns are the first sign of a customer at risk. While many customers may be ordering less due to the economic contraction, these changes need to be observed very carefully.
- Salespeople should work closely with their accounts receivable department to monitor for any changes in payment patterns, which can subtly indicate a possible credit problem.
- Industry trends and how they impact customers should be watched closely. Similar customers should be compared to determine whether patterns mirror one another.
- If major accounts are publicly traded, careful attention should be paid to quarterly profit projections found in the financial pages of newspapers and trade publications. The fact that many companies may be failing to meet their projections should trigger changes in the way accounts are handled.
- Salespeople should talk to others who call on the same customers, and actively trade information to keep on top of their accounts.
- Salespeople should also talk to other representatives in their own company who call on the same customers in other locations in order to keep each other appraised about the data and news collected.

- Salespeople who may have cultivated relationships with individuals who work for their major accounts should contact them frequently to find out any information regarding internal changes or shifts in trends.
- All sources of information should be monitored and pieced together to create a full picture of what might be occurring.

Competitive Risks

Competitive risks heat up during economic slowdowns. The fact that some vendors can act irrationally as they fight for their survival is further complicated by companies constantly introducing new products and technology as they struggle for a competitive edge. Salespeople must assume that their competition is actively pursuing their best customers. Below are indicators that point to a customer who is at a high competitive risk:

- In addition to a slowdown due to economic conditions, changes in purchasing patterns can also reflect competitive risks.
- Changes in the personal behaviors of buyers and decision makers should be noted. If a once-friendly contact suddenly avoids phone and/or personal contact, they are avoiding the salesperson for a reason.
- Changes in body language—if the buyer avoids eye contact, constantly fidgets or cuts meetings and conversations short—are indicative of a problem.
- Slowed decision making or an avoidance in making a commitment are also indicators that something is going on that the buyer does not wish to share with the salesperson.

Salespeople need to increase customer contact to protect their business. They need to look for evidence of product demonstrations and tests, and talk to as many people as possible to determine if the competition is succeeding in getting their foot in the door.

In both cases, salespeople need to be aware of what is happening and how it affects their customers and where possible, take immediate action to protect their business.

POINTS TO PONDER — SOMETHING TO THINK ABOUT

1. What changes have you observed in your territory over the past six months? What effects are those changes having on your customers?
2. Have you observed any changes in your competition's behavior? What have you done to counter them? Explain.

TRAINING ACTIVITY — APPLICATION & ACTION PLAN

Create a risk log for your territory.

1. Using the indicators listed above and any others you think are important, list all of the information you have collected for each major account.
2. Once completed, look for patterns that might point to a specific customer at risk.
3. If a customer is indicated, develop a strategy to recover this account before the business is lost.
4. Continue to maintain this log and review it at least twice a month.

4

Dealing with the Customer at Risk

At no point in time can salespeople ever assume that their business is completely safe. Major accounts are always at risk, and even more so during an economic slowdown, when competition intensifies as companies grapple with the economic realities of a recessionary market.

IMPLICATIONS – WHAT THIS MEANS TO YOU

Economic conditions heavily impact most salespeople. During a downturn—especially in the capital goods sector—many will experience a precipitous drop in performance. Pressure from sales managers to produce in the face of sagging market conditions further complicates the salesperson's life.

Salespeople have to develop proactive sales strategies to protect the business they have while exploring new markets to replace the losses produced by an economic downturn.

STRATEGIES, TIPS & TECHNIQUES TO APPLY

Salespeople cannot sit back and hope for the best, but must be aggressive in identifying their at-risk customers and prospects. Once they have done this, the following strategies can be used to buttress an existing account or recover one that is about to be lost.

Identify the Risk Factors

The initial step in identifying threatened accounts is to determine the risk factors affecting a specific customer. This includes confirming that the customer is actually at risk and not just a victim of slowing market conditions. Salespeople may need to confirm that the customer is being courted by a competitor and may be in the process of evaluating their products and services.

Confirm the Risk

Once salespeople have determined with some degree of certainty that their customer is at risk, they need to meet with the buyer to ascertain whether he or she is considering a competitive offer.

At this point the buyer should not be confronted, but deftly approached and asked whether or not they are considering a competitor's products or services.

Determine the Level of Risk

Once the buyer has confirmed that they are, in fact, considering other products and services, the salesperson will need to probe further to determine the level of risk. This includes identifying how far into the evaluation process the customer has proceeded and the results of their evaluation.

Additional information needs to be gathered, including how well the buyer likes the competitor's products and what is specifically liked or disliked in regard to them. This information will provide a basis for developing a counteroffer. Salespeople will also need to determine the price and other pertinent information if the buyer is willing to share it with them.

Identify the Problems and Issues

It is essential to probe to determine what prompted the buyer to consider the competition. Was there a specific problem with their products or service? What is the competition offering that the salesperson couldn't provide?

The customer is obviously dissatisfied with something to have opened the doors to the competition. Their business cannot be recovered until these problems and issues are brought into the open and resolved.

Identify Potential Solutions

Once answers to the four areas listed above have been collected, salespeople can craft a series of potential solutions for them. If there had been a previously established solid relationship and rapport with the buyer, it is likely their proposal will be carefully considered.

Gain Acceptance

If the buyer is open to solutions and recommendations, it is time to resell them on the reasons why they bought in the first place. Salespeople must use the good will developed over the term of the relationship to remind and resell the buyer on the benefits of continuing the sales relationship.

Seek Commitment

The final step is to resell the buyer and seek a commitment to remain with the company. During this process, new products and technologies may have to be introduced or pricing renegotiated. The buyer should see that the salesperson is willing to take the actions necessary to keep their business, solve their problems, and support their goals and objectives.

Salespeople need to trade on the value of their relationship with their customers. Unless a major problem has occurred to break the trust, they should have the inside track over a new competitor. Now is the time to pull out all of the stops to make sure the customer remains with the company.

POINTS TO PONDER — SOMETHING TO THINK ABOUT

1. What actions have you taken when identifying a customer at risk? Explain.
2. What success have you had in recovering lost or at-risk customers?

TRAINING ACTIVITY — APPLICATION & ACTION PLAN

1. Identify a potential customer who you feel may be at risk.
2. Develop a sales strategy to recover and reconfirm their commitment to you using the strategy listed above.

5

What to Do When You Lose a Sale

The salesperson has given it their best shot, and worked hard only to lose the sale to a competitor. Now what? There are specific things salespeople need to do to recover the relationship as quickly as possible if the customer is not to be permanently lost.

IMPLICATIONS — WHAT THIS MEANS TO YOU

All is not lost when a sale goes to the competition. The salesperson has invested their time and expertise in building a relationship. He or she may experience a temporary setback, but the relationship developed still exists.

Most salespeople will burn their bridges and move on. They take the loss as a personal insult rather than the business decision it is. This is a major mistake. Needs change, new opportunities continually evolve and develop, individuals change jobs and priorities shift. No matter what happens, salespeople continuing to foster the relationship will pay dividends in the long term.

STRATEGIES, TIPS & TECHNIQUES TO APPLY

When a salesperson loses an order, the buyer knows they have disappointed them. Because of this fact, if it is within their power to do so, the next time they are more likely to favor them with an order.

The key is for salespeople to continually keep their options open and always give the customer incentives to come back. Negative emotional reactions build hostility and often work to prevent the customer from returning, even when they wish to do so.

Specific proven techniques will ensure that lines of communication remain open and leave the impression with the customer that they will always be welcome to return:

- Salespeople should check in with their prospect after the competition has delivered their product or service to question how things went and if their expectations have been met. If the competition over-promised and under-delivered, the door may be open once again. Visits should be kept friendly and upbeat, as the purpose is to maintain the relationship and keep the avenues of communication open.
- From time to time, salespeople should send the prospect interesting articles and information about their company and industry. A note is attached indicating how the information applies to their business.
- Keeping in touch with the customer positions salespeople for new and unexpected opportunities. People prefer to buy from those they like. If the customer feels badly about giving their business to a competitor, they may be seeking ways to reopen the door as new and additional opportunities present themselves.

POINTS TO PONDER — SOMETHING TO THINK ABOUT

1. How do you react to the loss of an order? Do you view it as a personal affront or a business decision?
2. Are you able to separate yourself from negative emotions and maintain a relationship with the prospect or customer? What do you do to keep the relationship and your reactions professional? Is there anything you need to improve upon?

TRAINING ACTIVITY — APPLICATION & ACTION PLAN

Develop a customer recovery program.

1. Determine the immediate actions you need to take when a customer leaves you for a competitor.
   a. What is your immediate response?
   b. What options will be available to you?
   c. What actions do you need to take?
2. If the customer leaves, how will you foster and maintain the relationship?
3. Develop a concrete plan and commit it to writing. Place it in your files for ready reference to prevent you from emotionally reacting to the situation.

6

Identifying the Reasons Behind a Lost Sale

Many salespeople are surprised when they lose a major customer. When this occurs it is critical to discover the main reasons for the loss, first, in order to prevent them from occurring again, and second, to provide insight into ways to get the business back.

IMPLICATIONS – WHAT THIS MEANS TO YOU

An examination of the causes behind the loss of business indicates in many instances how the salesperson could have prevented it by either paying closer attention or taking action to resolve a nagging problem.

There are times when a loss can be caused by a lack of sales and customer support on the part of the company. It is important to identify these problems and address them before they result in the loss of additional business.

In order to preserve their base of business, salespeople must take the time to foster and nurture their existing customers. This means developing a customer focus rather than concentrating on their own need to get the next sale. If the salesperson fails to protect their customers, their competition will. In many cases, it is important to fight for the customer. One way is to immediately rectify any pressing problems.

STRATEGIES, TIPS & TECHNIQUES TO APPLY

There are a number of factors that contribute to a loss of business for both a prospective and existing customer. These include:

Prospective Customers

Failure to Identify the Prospect's Needs – The salesperson has failed to adequately identify the prospect's needs and craft a solution that addresses these needs. The prospect fails to understand that the solution offered will adequately meet their needs.

Failure to Educate the Prospect About the Value of the Product – The prospect has not been educated about the value that the product can provide to them and therefore evaluates the product on the basis of price alone.

Failure to Establish the Value of the Product – Because the salesperson has failed to establish the value of their product, the customer only evaluates the product from the perspective of price.

Existing Customers

Damaged Customer Relationship – The trust and rapport between the customer and the salesperson has been broken. Additional reasons may stem from the customer forming a strong dislike for the salesperson.

Quality Problems – The product the customer has been purchasing has developed quality problems they refuse to accept since they may impact their productivity, efficiency and profitability.

Service Problems – Problems with delivery, technical assistance or customer service may have caused a continual source of frustration. When the frustration is not addressed, the customer has no other recourse than to fix the problem by changing suppliers.

Changing Needs – The customer's needs have changed and evolved and the salesperson either cannot meet their new needs or has failed to identify them.

Technological Advances – The competition has introduced a new product that provides superior technological advancements to that of the product the customer has been using.

Price Issues – The competition has provided a similar product at a lower price.

A Nagging Unresolved Problem – No customer expects their vendor to be perfect. However, when a problem arises, they do expect a quick and timely response. When the problem remains unsolved, the customer becomes increasingly hostile, ultimately to the point where they will bring in a new supplier to resolve the problem.

POINTS TO PONDER – SOMETHING TO THINK ABOUT

1. When have you lost an account? Where specifically have you placed the blame for the loss?
2. What actions are you taking to protect your customer's business?

TRAINING ACTIVITY – APPLICATION & ACTION PLAN

Identify one or more major customer problems you are currently experiencing and the major pieces of business you have lost in the past six months.

1. Using the criteria listed above, determine the primary causes for the lost business.
2. Determine whether there was anything you could have done to prevent the loss.
3. Based upon your findings, identify specific actions and strategies you can employ to recover the business.

7

Crafting a Solution to Regain Lost Business

Because there are specific reasons why a customer decides to change suppliers, it is imperative that a salesperson responds quickly when business is lost. It is equally important to identify the causes behind the loss and craft a solution in an attempt to recover the account. A failure to adequately and promptly respond can result in a permanent loss of the account and a perceived admission that the customer was right in their decision to change.

IMPLICATIONS — WHAT THIS MEANS TO YOU

Losing a customer places salespeople in a precarious position. How and when they craft an appropriate response has an impact on their ability to recover the business. An emotional response can place the customer in a defensive posture. A response that is too relaxed can create the perception that the salesperson doesn't care. No response at all reinforces that the customer made the right decision to leave.

The appropriate response is timely, identifies the problem behind the loss, and provides the customer with an acceptable solution. It provides the customer with an additional option and creates a question in their mind as to whether or not they are making the best choice.

STRATEGIES, TIPS & TECHNIQUES TO APPLY

Previous chapters have covered the specific reasons why a customer may choose to change suppliers. The first step salespeople must take is to identify the problem(s) and issue(s) surrounding the decision to change. In many cases the factors surrounding the decision to change are symptomatic of a deeper problem. Rather than accept the customer's initial explanation, salespeople must probe for additional information to help them identify the root causes. Often this takes time and the use of salespeople's expertise and experience to analyze what is causing the customer to select a new supplier. Typically, problems can be classified into three main areas:

- Quality Problems
- Service Problems
- Price Problems

Once salespeople have isolated the root causes behind a problem, they need to determine the reasons it occurred in the first place. This can be classified into five main categories:

- Misuse or misapplication of the product by the customer
- A problem caused by poor product or service quality
- A problem caused by poor service by the company
- A problem caused by the poor service of the salesperson
- A perception of a problem created by the competition

Once the primary cause of the problem has been identified, solutions can be created to solve it. In most cases the cause of the problem is beyond the control of the salesperson. In these situations, salespeople must access the resources available to them to develop a number of potential solutions. Using the input from management, production and other areas, ideas for solutions can be brainstormed and developed.

As the timing of the solution is important, getting to the point of identifying the best solution must be performed quickly. Additionally, salespeople must use their expertise and experience to gauge how to craft a specific solution in such a way that the customer is most receptive. There is no ideal answer, and the customer's temperament, emotional state and receptiveness to a solution must all be taken into consideration.

POINTS TO PONDER – SOMETHING TO THINK ABOUT

1. How have you crafted a response to lost business in the past? How would you describe your response and the customer's reaction?
2. Have you ever overreacted to a customer's decision to go with another supplier? What was the customer's response or actions? Did you learn a specific lesson from this experience? Explain.

TRAINING ACTIVITY – APPLICATION & ACTION PLAN

Identify a current customer problem or one that you recently experienced.

1. Examine your response to the problem and compare it to the approach listed above.
2. Contrast your approach against the recommended approach in this lesson.
3. Determine what additional steps you need to take to resolve the problem.

8

Strategies to Recover a Lost Account

Customers will change suppliers for a host of reasons. The salesperson is responsible for recapturing the lost business and may face a variety of situations that need to be dealt with before a customer's business can be recovered. A one-size-fits-all approach to this problem is not appropriate. Instead, the salesperson must become an analyst to determine the best approach to recover the business.

IMPLICATIONS – WHAT THIS MEANS TO YOU

Recovery of a lost account will take all of the skills, expertise, knowledge, resources and experience the salesperson can muster. They must know exactly how to deal with each individual situation and customer. With each situation, the parameters will change as will the dynamics of the people involved, and the salesperson must walk a fine line. In its basic form, recovery of a customer's business translates into reestablishing broken trust and rapport. The salesperson may feel betrayed by the customer's actions, but must put these feelings aside if they are to be successful.

STRATEGIES, TIPS & TECHNIQUES TO APPLY

Once a customer is actually lost, recovery can be tricky. After the salesperson has gone through the process of identifying the underlying causes behind the problem and taken the time to craft a specific solution, he or she has the tools to begin the recovery of the account. There is no general approach to apply when attempting to recover an account. The individual approach must rely on the personality and mindset of the customer. Detailed below are five of the most common personalities and the approach to use for each.

The Indifferent Customer

The indifferent customer doesn't care one way or another who supplies them. These are individuals who may view all products as commodities and, as such, only evaluate a product on the basis of price. They are either ignorant or indifferent about the quality and the value of the product they are buying. In these instances the salesperson probably has failed to establish a personal relationship of trust and rapport. The initial business may have come easily because the price was right, but now the customer has jumped to an even lower-cost provider.

An indifferent customer doesn't provide the salesperson with a lot of options. Since they are indifferent, the salesperson cannot rely on past relationships to begin their recovery attempts. The best approach is to identify what this type of customer actually cares about, which is typically price. If the account is worthwhile, the only approach is to build the solution accordingly. As quickly as they jumped to a competitor, they will jump back if it is to their advantage.

The Reluctant Customer

The reluctant customer had a good relationship with the salesperson, but for various reasons felt compelled to make a change in suppliers. Because they have a strong sense of loyalty to the salesperson, when approached, these individuals might feel sheepish or embarrassed by their decision.

Reluctant customers are more receptive to a counteroffer and willing to give the salesperson a chance to get the business back. The salesperson must use the past relationship as a starting point, leveraging the customer's guilt to their advantage. They must remind this type of customer of all the positive things he or she liked about them and their product or service. The salesperson should emphasize the strong relationship that is established against the unknowns of a new relationship with a different vendor.

The Arrogant Customer

The arrogant customer will be proud of his or her decision to switch vendors and act as if a victory has been achieved over the salesperson. For one reason or another these individuals are compelled to gain the upper hand; the salesperson is dealing with control issues and an inflated ego. Because these customers are master game players, the salesperson has to use their skills to outthink them.

If the salesperson is to recover the account, he or she must feed the customer's ego. As any direct confrontation with this type of individual will result in a permanent loss of their business, the salesperson must be subtle in their approach. Recommendations must be suggested in such a way that the customer thinks they are his or her idea and thus can take the credit. Due to the explosive nature of the situation, the salesperson needs to proceed with caution and one step at a time until the account is recovered.

The Hostile Customer

The hostile customer is frustrated by something the salesperson or their company has failed to address. Because they had unmet expectations—even if those expectations were unrealistic—they felt the only option available to them was to change suppliers.

The recovery process cannot proceed until all of the underlying issues are resolved to the customer's satisfaction. Salespeople must ensure that the hostile customer's source of frustration is removed, no matter how minor it may appear.

Timely actions, not words, must have the utmost priority at this time. If the customer has unmet expectations, that issue must also be addressed. The salesperson must identify the basis of their expectations and correct any misperceptions. Additionally, they must provide assurances to demonstrate that the problem will not recur. This is the only way that the customer's trust can be reestablished.

The Angry Customer

The angry customer has been pushed to the point of utter frustration by the actions of either the salesperson or their company. Something probably occurred that negatively impacted their profitability and productivity—in many instances a product or delivery failure coupled with inaction or indifference on the part of the salesperson.

In this situation the salesperson is clearly facing an uphill battle. The first thing that must be addressed is the customer's anger. At this point, it is difficult to see eye to eye with the customer: they feel that every opportunity was provided to the salesperson to initially resolve the problem, and they failed. In many cases, sales or other company managers may have to initially intervene to allow the customer to vent and then resolve the problem to their satisfaction. If this is not possible, the salesperson may have no other recourse than to allow the customer time to cool their emotions and then approach the situation at a later date.

POINTS TO PONDER — SOMETHING TO THINK ABOUT

1. When encountering a problem, have you taken the customer's mindset into consideration? Explain.
2. What specific customer mindsets have you experienced? What were the results of your encounters?

TRAINING ACTIVITY — APPLICATION & ACTION PLAN

Identify a current customer problem you are experiencing or one that recently occurred.

1. Identify the type of customer you are dealing with as described above.

2. Determine whether the approach you are using is appropriate to the customer type.
3. Identify ways to modify your approach that is appropriate for the customer you are dealing with.

About the Author

Timothy F. Bednarz, Ph.D. is CEO of the American Management Development Group, Inc. For over 20 years he has researched, designed and authored hundreds of learning and development programs used by Fortune 1000 companies.

He is also the author of *Great! What Makes Leaders Great. What They Did, How They Did It and What You Can Learn from It* (2011).

Speaking Availability

Timothy F. Bednarz, Ph.D. is available for speaking engagements for your next meeting or association event. He can be contacted at 800-654-4935 or by e-mail at timothy.bednarz@majorium.com.

Bulk Sales

Bulk sales of this book or any other titles available from Majorium Business Press. Inquiries can be directed to sales@majorium.com, or by phone at 800-6654-4935.

Quick Order Form

Fax orders: 715-342-1118. Send this form.

Telephone orders: Call 800-654-4935 toll-free. Have your credit card ready.

Email orders: sales@majorium.com

Postal orders: Majorium Business Press, 2025 Main Street, Stevens Point, WI 54481, USA.

Please send the following books:

____

____

____

____

Please send more FREE information on:

❑ Catalog ❑ Speaking/Seminars ❑ Mailing Lists ❑ Consulting

Name: ____________________________________

Address: __________________________________

City: ____________________ State: _____ Zip: __________

Telephone: ________________________________

Email address: ______________________________

Sales tax: Please add 5.5% for products shipped to Wisconsin addresses.

Shipping by air:

United States: $4.00 for first book and $2.00 for each additional product.

International: $9.00 for first book; $5.00 for each additional product (estimate).

Made in United States
Cleveland, OH
06 November 2026

47678346R10026